Amazing Animal Homes

G000059393

Tamara Einstein &
Einstein Sisters

KidsWorld

Types of Homes

Eastern Bluebird with
Nesting Material

Animals of all
kinds make homes for
themselves. Homes
can be nests, burrows,
lodges or webs.

Some homes are
used by the animal for
its whole life, while other
homes are made new each
year. Homes can also be
built for just one stage of
an animal's life.

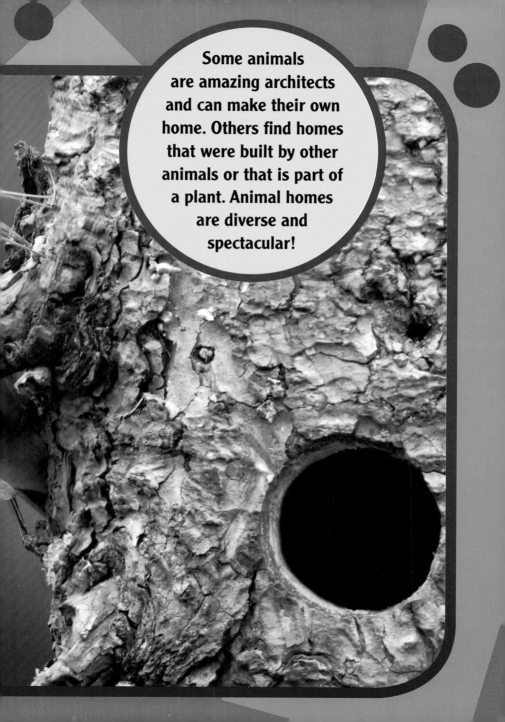

Some animals are amazing architects and can make their own home. Others find homes that were built by other animals or that is part of a plant. Animal homes are diverse and spectacular!

Sociable Weaver Bird

The sociable weaver bird is a kind of sparrow that lives in southern Africa. These birds live in large groups that make a single, permanent nest with many openings and chambers.

The nest of a group of sociable weavers is the largest structure made by any bird. One large nest may be home to more than 100 pairs of birds. The inner chambers keep heat in at night, while the outer chambers stay cool in the shade and breeze during the day.

Sociable Weaver at Entrance

One nest may be home to many generations of birds. Other birds, such as finches, may nest within the large nest too. Owls, falcons and vultures may nest on top of the sociable weaver bird's nest!

Acacia Ant

The acacia ant lives only on acacia trees. The ants and the tree benefit from each other. The colony starts with a single queen. She chews a hole in a thorn and lays eggs inside it. The eggs hatch, and the larvae grow.

Hole Made by Ants

As the colony of ants grows, they make holes in more and more of the thorns on the tree. A large colony in a single tree can have several thousand ants!

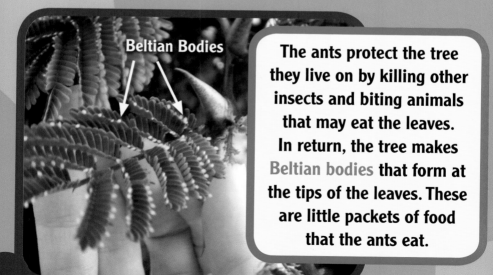

Beltian Bodies

The ants protect the tree they live on by killing other insects and biting animals that may eat the leaves. In return, the tree makes Beltian bodies that form at the tips of the leaves. These are little packets of food that the ants eat.

Beaver

Beavers Eating Tree Bark

Beavers are the second-largest rodent in the world. They gnaw at tree bases to bring them down so they can use the wood to make dams and lodges.

A beaver lodge has entrances underwater. The center of the lodge is above the water so the beavers have a safe, warm place to live.

Inside a Beaver Lodge

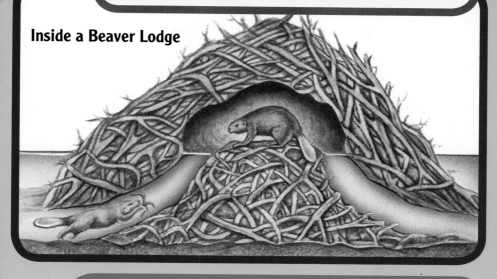

Beavers can change the landscape by making dams in streams and rivers to make pools of water. Beavers need deep pools in which to build their lodges.

Beaver Dam

Termites

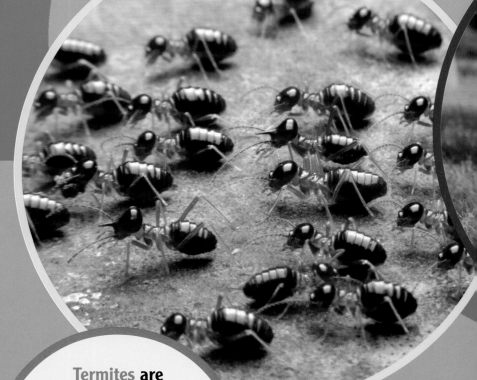

Termites are extremely social insects. They live in groups of a few hundred to a few million individuals. Termites make nests in trees or on the ground.

Termite Mounds

Some termite species build large mounds on the ground. The shape of the mounds and the network of tunnels within it control the inside humidity and temperature for the colony.

Termites build their mounds using soil and clay. Passageways in the mound lead to a central underground nest where eggs and larvae grow.

Termites Inside Their Nest

Wasp

Wasp is a general term for several species of insects, including the common wasp, several yellowjackets and the bald-faced hornet. Wasps make large, papery nests.

Bald-faced Hornet

Large Wasp Nest

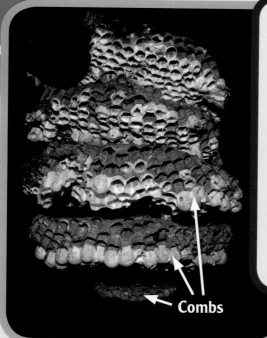

Combs

Inside the wasp nest are layers of combs. Each chamber of the combs holds an egg that was laid by the queen. The egg hatches into a larva. The larva stays in its chamber and is fed by the worker wasps until it is ready to pupate and become an adult.

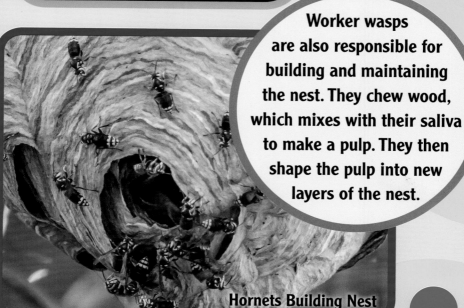

Worker wasps are also responsible for building and maintaining the nest. They chew wood, which mixes with their saliva to make a pulp. They then shape the pulp into new layers of the nest.

Hornets Building Nest

Baya Weaver

The baya weaver is a small bird that lives in Asia and India. The hanging woven nests of this weaver have long funnels that lead to the nest chamber. The nest design is effective at stopping most predators from entering and eating the eggs and chicks.

Baya Weaver Flying to Nest

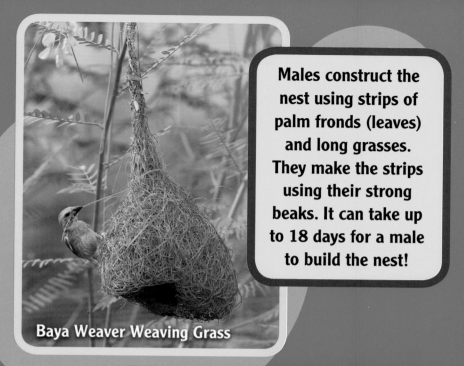

Baya Weaver Weaving Grass

Males construct the nest using strips of palm fronds (leaves) and long grasses. They make the strips using their strong beaks. It can take up to 18 days for a male to build the nest!

Baya weavers prefer to nest in colonies. Females choose a male based on the quality of the nest he has built.

Nest Colony

Hummingbirds

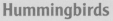

Hummingbirds make nests that are a little different than the nests of most other birds. To make their nests, they use strands of spider silk. They collect the silk from spiderwebs.

The nest is tiny, just large enough to hold the female and her egg.

When the egg hatches, the chick grows quickly. The spider silk nest is a bit stretchy, so the nest can grow as the chick does!

Funnel Weaving Spiders

Spiders produce silk, and most spiders spin some kind of web. Funnel weaving spiders make webs that have a cone shape, like a funnel. The spiders feed on insects that fall into the web and tumble down into the center.

Funnel Web in Grass

Spider Waiting

At the bottom of the funnel is a burrow. The spider lives in the burrow and emerges when its prey struggles in the web. These spiders run extremely fast. They dart out to catch their prey and race back to their burrow.

Side View of Funnel Web

There are many kinds of spiders that make funnel webs. Some have venom that is dangerous to humans.

Trapdoor Spiders

Several types of spiders make burrows lined with silk that have a special lid or trapdoor. They are called trapdoor spiders. They make the lid using silk to stick together bits of dirt, sand, dry twigs and grass. The inside of the lid is usually padded with extra silk.

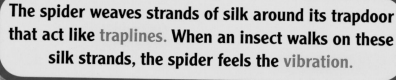

The spider weaves strands of silk around its trapdoor that act like traplines. When an insect walks on these silk strands, the spider feels the vibration.

Tips of the Spider's Claws

To catch its prey, the spider pushes the lid open, grabs the insect with its front legs and pulls it into the burrow, all in less than a second!

Snails

Snails are also called shelled gastropods, and they can be found in saltwater, freshwater and on land. Snails make a shell that protects them. They cannot leave their shell.

Rose Bubble Snail

Grape Snail

Incomplete Shell

Shells made by snails are mainly calcium and protein. As the snail grows, the shell is secreted in layers by a special organ called the mantle. Once the snail has reached full size, the outer edge of the shell thickens to prevent chipping.

Completed Shell

Snails with a single shell make a "door" called an operculum. They can retreat into their shell and close the door! Snails with two shells, such as clams, can close their two shells together for protection.

Operculum

Some species of snails are tiny, while others can be quite large. The largest univalve (snail with one shell) is the Australian trumpet. It can be 90 centimeters (3 feet) long! The giant clam is the largest bivalve (snail with two shells). It can be 120 centimeters (4 feet) long and weigh as much as a piano!

Australian Trumpet

Giant Clam

Hermit crabs are small crustaceans that use empty snails shells as their homes. Although they are called crabs, they have long bodies, more like lobsters. Their long bodies can wrap inside a spiral shell.

Hermit Crab in Transparent Shell

Hermit crabs are able to retreat into their shells. Their long body is soft, and the shell protects them.

Hermit Crab Hiding in Shell

As a hermit crab grows, it needs to find larger and larger shells to live in. It leaves its own shell to inspect an empty shell. If the emtpy shell is too big, it waits for many hours for another crab to show up. If the next hermit crab fits the new shell better, the first one will take the second one's abandoned shell.

Sometimes hermit crabs wait at a large empty shell and form a long vacancy chain by holding onto each other in order from biggest to smallest. They wait for the crab that best fits the large empty shell. When the right size crab arrives, they all quickly switch shells down the line, each hermit crab getting the slightly larger shell of the crab it was holding onto.

Hermit Crabs

Prairie Dogs

Prairie dogs are a kind of ground squirrel that live in large groups. They are sociable, and they often groom and kiss each other.

Prairie Dog Town

Prairie dog groups live in complex burrow systems called towns. A town can extend for many hectares (acres). Underground, the burrows have nest chambers, toilet chambers, food storage areas and emergency exits for when predators such as snakes enter the town.

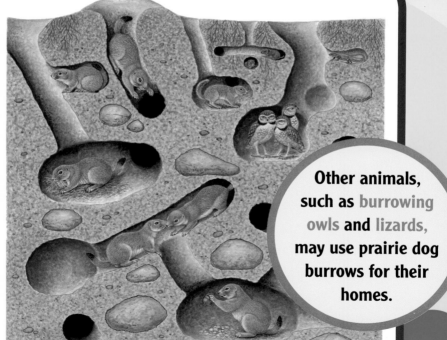

Other animals, such as burrowing owls and lizards, may use prairie dog burrows for their homes.

Cross section of Prairie Dog Burrow

Burrowing Owls

Burrowing owls **are the only** birds of prey **that live in burrows. They usually live in vacated burrows excavated by prairie dogs or other animals, but they can also dig their own.**

When threatened, a burrowing owl hides in its burrow and makes a hissing sound. This sound resembles a rattlesnake and may scare away the threat.

Cross section of Burrow

A female owl lays her eggs in the nest chamber of the burrow. Her owlets hatch underground and emerge from the burrow when they are about 4 weeks old.

Owls may leave bits of animal poo around the entrance to their burrow and inside the nest chamber. The poo attracts bugs that the owls love to eat!

Bagworm Moths

The larvae of bagworm moths construct elaborate homes, called bags or cases. One species, called the log cabin bagworm, makes a little home out of cut sticks that resembles a log cabin!

Various species of bagworm moths make their cases out of different materials. The larvae bind sticks, bits of leaves, lichen or sand with silk that they spin to make their cases.

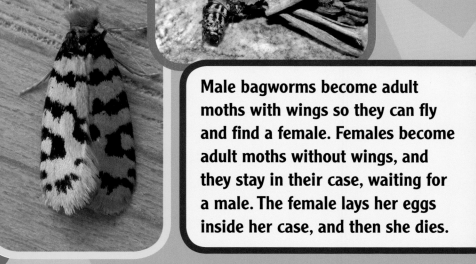

Male bagworms become adult moths with wings so they can fly and find a female. Females become adult moths without wings, and they stay in their case, waiting for a male. The female lays her eggs inside her case, and then she dies.

Burrowing Penguins

Although penguins are usually thought of as living at the south pole, several penguin species are found in warm climates such as South America, Africa, Australia and New Zealand.

Magellanic Penguins

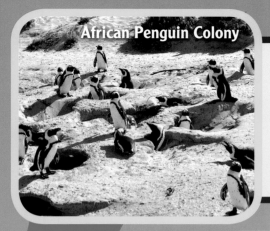
African Penguin Colony

Burrowing penguins live in large colonies for safety. Males and females bond for life, and use their same burrow each year.

Females lay one or two eggs in a burrow and incubate them until they hatch. Chicks are fuzzy until their adult feathers grow in.

Magellanic Penguin with Chicks

Magellanic Penguins in Burrow

When penguins molt their feathers, they cannot go into the water. They need their shadey burrows to stay cool in hot climates.

False Burnet Moths

False burnet moths **are rather plain as adults, but the larva (caterpillar) makes an amazing home for itself.**

upa in its Case Woven
ith Silk and Grass

Pupa in its Case

The larvae construct their delicate woven homes out of the silk they spin. When the casing is finished, the larva inside becomes a pupa. During this phase the pupa looks dead, but it is transforming into an adult moth.

Pupa in its Case

Adult Moth

Diving Bell Spider

The diving bell spider is the only spider in the world that lives underwater. Like all other spiders, it needs to breathe air, so it makes a special air bubble home called a bell. The bell is held underwater by webbing attached to plants. The spider makes the bell by going to the surface and bringing air trapped in the hairs on its abdomen. It releases the air into the growing bell.

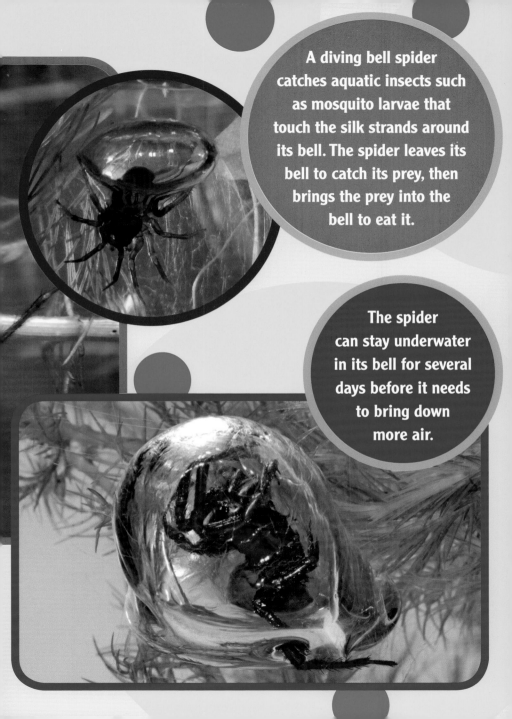

A diving bell spider catches aquatic insects such as mosquito larvae that touch the silk strands around its bell. The spider leaves its bell to catch its prey, then brings the prey into the bell to eat it.

The spider can stay underwater in its bell for several days before it needs to bring down more air.

Cliff Swallow

Cliff swallows are small birds that feed on flying insects. They make nests out of clay mud that they collect from ditches, puddles, lakes or rivers.

Cliff Swallow

To build a nest, males and females collect bits of mud in their mouths. They use these clay blobs like bricks, laying them down one by one. The nest takes 1 to 2 weeks to complete.

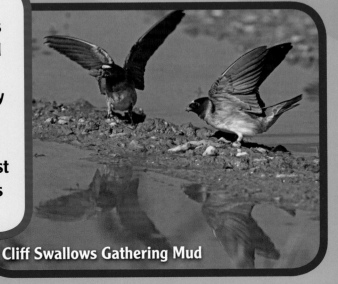

Cliff Swallows Gathering Mud

Cliff Swallows in their Nests

Gourds

Cliff swallows are extremely social birds and live in large groups called colonies. They build their gourd-shaped nests in clusters for better support. The largest colonies have more than 2000 nests!

Cliff Swallow Colony

Potter Wasp

Potter wasps are a large group of wasp species, most of which make nests that resemble tiny clay pots. Potter wasps are solitary, meaning they live alone.

The female collects mud in her mouth and uses it to form her nest. Some potter wasps use chewed-up plant material instead of mud. A female may make one pot nest or several.

Potter Wasp Building Nest

Potter Wasp Nest

When the nest is nearly finished, the female catches an insect, spider or caterpillar to place inside. She then lays a single egg in the nest. Once the egg is laid, she closes up the opening of the nest.

Potter Wasp Nests

The egg hatches, and the wasp larva feeds on the trapped prey. After the larva eats its prey, it pupates. The new adult wasp chews its way out of the nest.

Wild Hogs

Wild hogs are escaped pigs or wild boar. They are found around the world. Recently, wild hogs are increasing in numbers in parts of central North America with cold winters. These hogs have learned a neat trick to beat the cold.

To survive cold winters, a wild hog makes a large pile of snow mixed with cut cattails. On cold days, the hog burrows into its "pigloo" where it stays warm.

Piglets can be born any time of the year. They are striped like chipmunks!

Wild hogs eat just about anything, including plants, roots, fruits, mushrooms, eggs, reptiles, birds and small mammals.

Arboreal Ants

Arboreal Ant

Unlike most ants, arboreal ants make their nests in trees. Their nests are made of chewed plant material. Some species of arboreal ants rarely even leave the tree in which they live.

Arboreal Ant Nest

Many arboreal ants have developed the ability to glide. If they fall from the nest or from a tree branch, they can glide and turn in the air so they can land on the trunk of their tree. If they land on the ground, they are less likely to be able to find their way back to the nest.

Arboreal Ant Nest

Harvest Mouse

The unusual harvest mouse lives in Europe and Asia. Unlike other mice that live in ground nests, the harvest mouse makes its nest in bushes!

A female harvest mouse makes her round grass nest among cattails, corn crops, thistles or other sturdy plants.

A female makes a new nest for each litter of pups she gives birth to—up to three per year. Each litter can have up to eight pups!

Edible Nest Swiftlets

Black Nest Swiftlet

Edible nest swiftlets are birds that make nests that humans can eat. Swiftlets make their nests in caves and sometimes in buildings.

The tiny nest is about the size of a child's hand, and the swiftlet makes it from its own saliva! Their saliva is rich in protein. Layers upon layers of saliva harden to make the nest. Soaking the nest in water makes it come apart into strands, like noodles.

Bird's nest soup is considered a delicacy in Chinese cooking.

Oropendola

Oropendolas are birds that live in Central and South America. Although there are several species, each species has bright yellow feathers in its tail. Oropendolas make their nests in colonies in trees.

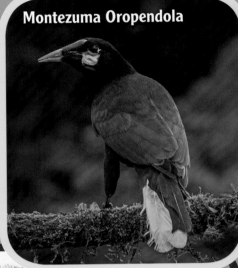

Montezuma Oropendola

Oropendola Nests

A female builds
her nest out of grass,
vines and other long fibers.
She lays two eggs in the
nest, and she incubates
them without the help of
the male.

Nests can be
more than a meter
(3 feet) long! They
hang from the tips
of tree branches
high above the
forest floor.

Army Ants

Army Ants in a Bivouac

Army ants build one of the most unique homes in the animal world. They build a home with their own bodies! The nest is called a bivouac and is formed by the ants holding onto each other's legs. Most of the ants leave the bivouac during the day to find food for the larvae. When the larvae become pupae they can be moved to a new bivouac site with new food sources.

Army Ants Forming a Bivouac

An army ant bivouac has passageways and chambers for food, larvae, eggs and the queen. While foraging ants leave the bivouac during the day, some ants stay to maintain the chambers that house the queen and the larvae.

Inside a Bivouac

Rufous Hornero

Clay Oven

The **rufous hornero** is a bird that lives in South America. It makes clay nests that resemble traditional clay ovens. The name **hornero** comes from *horno,* which is Spanish for **oven.**

Both the male and female work together to build the nest, carrying mud in their mouths to the nest site. The nest takes about 5 days to complete.

The nest has a spiral entrance, a bit like a seashell. This helps protect the eggs and young birds from predators like snakes, lizards and cats.

Both male and female incubate the eggs and care for their young. They eat insects and spiders, which they also feed to their chicks.

Caddisfly Larva

The caddisfly is a large group of insects, and it has larvae that live underwater. The larvae make tubular homes, using silk and bits of plants, sand, seeds and other small objects. Various species of caddisflies use different types of materials to make their homes.

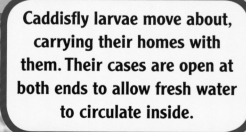

Caddisfly larvae move about, carrying their homes with them. Their cases are open at both ends to allow fresh water to circulate inside.

The larvae pupate in the cases, meaning they become dormant and transform into adults. When the adult emerges, it has to swim to the surface and leave the water. An adult caddisfly resembles a small moth.

Caddis Fly Adult

One species of caddisfly uses empty snail shells to build its home!

Bowerbird

Bowerbirds create fancy bowers out of grass or twigs. A **bower** is a shady place or structure. Male bowerbirds build their bowers and decorate them with flowers, feathers, shells, berries, seeds or bits of plastic or glass.

A male satin bowerbird has a strong preference for blue objects. The older a male gets, the more blue objects he collects and displays.

Satin Bowerbird

Vogelkop Bowerbird in Bower

The male Vogelkop bowerbird makes a large bower out of twigs. He places colorful objects in piles in his bower to attract a female.

Weaver ants work together to make a nest of leaves woven together with silk from their larvae.

Reaching for a Leaf

Pulling a Leaf Closer

After they pull a leaf into position, the workers hold onto it tightly. Other worker ants bring larvae from other nests so they can produce silk to "glue" the leaf in place.

Holding a Leaf in Place

Weaver Ant Nest

Weaver Ant Nest

One nest takes about a day to build. The completed nest looks like a ball of leaves. One colony of ants can make hundreds of nests in many trees. The nests are waterproof and strong.

Weaver Ants

Three-spined Stickleback

The three-spined stickleback is a kind of minnow (small fish) that lives in sheltered coastal waters. Unlike most other fish, male sticklebacks make nests out of plant material.

After the male constructs his nest, he swims in a zig-zag pattern around his nest to attract a female. If a female chooses the male, she will lay her eggs in the nest.

As the eggs develop, the male fans the nest with his fins to keep clean water flowing over the eggs. When they hatch, the male keeps the fry (baby fish) in the nest for a few days by sucking up wanderers in his mouth and spitting them back into the nest.

© 2019 KidsWorld Books
Printed in China

The Publisher: KidsWorld Books

Library and Archives Canada Cataloguing in Publication

Title: Amazing animal homes / Tamara Einstein & Einstein Sisters.
Names: Einstein, Tamara, author. | Einstein Sisters, author.

Identifiers: Canadiana (print) 20200201247 | Canadiana (ebook) 20200201255 | ISBN 9781988183565 (softcover) | ISBN 9781988183572 (PDF)

Subjects: LCSH: Animals—Habitations—Juvenile literature.

Classification: LCC QL756 .E56 2020 | DDC j591.56/4—dc23

Front cover: From Getty Images: Baya Weaver by Syed F Abbas.

Back cover: Log Cabin Bagworm Moth Larva by Chien C. Lee; Rufous Hornero by Tamara Hartson; Rose Bubble Snail by Samuel Chow, Wikimedia Commons.

Photo credits: From Wikimedia Commons: © 2009 Jee & Rani Nature Photography 19a; Alexander Mrkvicka 31c; Baupi 36; Beatriz Moisset 12a; Bruce Marlin 40a; dhobern 31d; Geoff Gallice 34, 52a, 53; Guglielmo Celata 33b; Ilia Ustyantsev 35c; Jacy Lucier 44a; João Medeiros 16; Katja Schulz 57b; Marcelcvaz 35b; MOHAN LAL MOURYA 15b; Mounty 64a 56; Olga Ernst 33a; Philip N. Cohen 13b; Pratheepps 44b; Rama Warrier 40b; Ryan Somma 6a; Samuel Chow 22a; Valdison Aparecido Gil 51; Wasrts 13a. From Getty Images: 12MN 50b; Anest 41b; Atelopus 35a; barbaraaaa 17ab; Bharath Reddy 61a; bonchan 23a; BrianLasenby 12; BruceCampos 8b; casch 39c; Cheng_Wei 11b; clickclick1 60a; cwinegarden 33c; Daniel Mortell 24b; David Butler 27a; Dorling Kindersley 9a, 27b, 29b; DoucetPh 8a; Eshma 22c; finchfocus 49a; fputruele 54; frank600 60b; GroblerduPreez 5b; Hajakely 45; HenkBentlage 26b; Hongchanstudio 49b; jacobeukman 5a; Jef Wodniack 9b; Jeffrey Hamilton 25; JensenChua 11a; JeremyRichards 42-43, 43; jon841 23b; Ken Griffiths 59a; kuenlin 24a; MarcosMartinezSanchez 54; Maurizio Lanini 4; MikeLane45 47ab; nameinfame 39a; Noppharat05081977 60c; Oxford Scientific 46, 57c; Pedro_Turrini 28a; photographybyJHWilliams 38b; photosbyjim 26a; phototrip 57a; pong6400 10; Serg_Velusceac 39b; shakzu 7a; skeat 58; skodonnell 22d; SteveByland 2-3; treetstreet 23c; tribal-warrior 61b; Utopia_88 14; Uwe-Bergwitz 28b, 54; werajoe 15a; yogesh_more 31a; Yuriy_Kulik 22b; Zoonar RF 41c. From Flickr: Andy Morffew 50a; Bernard Dupont 31e, 53a; Bob Henricks 56b; Dinesh Valke 19b; Feroze Omardeen 6b; Francesco Veronesi 38a; kafka4prez 7b; Katja Schulz 41a; Marshal Hedin 20, 21ab; Pavel Kirillov 52; Tom Lee 18; Tomas Maul 31b; UW News 63ab; wokoti 48. From Alamy: Barrie Britton 59b; blickwinkel 37b. Other: aleo79 (Getty Images)/Charles Knowles (Flickr) 29a; Chien C. Lee 30; Roger Seymour 37a; Tamara Hartson 32, 55abc.

We acknowledge the financial support of the Government of Canada.
Nous reconnaissons l'appui financier du gouvernement du Canada.

Funded by the Government of Canada
Financé par le gouvernement du Canada | Canadä